Ac

The Ultimate Guide to Accounting for Beginners – Learn the Basic Accounting Principles

This book is for entertainment purposes only. The views expressed are those of the author alone, and should not be taken as expert instruction or commands. The reader is responsible for his or her own actions.

Adherence to all applicable laws and regulations, including international, federal, state and local laws governing professional licensing, business practices, advertising and all other aspects of doing business in the US, Canada, UK or any other jurisdiction is the sole responsibility of the purchaser or reader.

Neither the author nor the publisher assumes any responsibility or liability whatsoever on the behalf of the purchaser or reader of these materials. Any perceived slight of any individual or organization is purely unintentional.

Contents

Introduction

This book is intended for people who want to know something about the fundamentals of financial accounting without becoming an accountant. Many people are in this position; small business owners, employers, employees, business owners, stockholders, investors, and many, many more. Most of these folks do not need a deep understanding of accounting, they just need to learn what accounting is and how they should be using it. Just as important, they need to understand what accountants are talking about in their reports. They must learn the vocabulary and the most important terms. The product of accounting is information, important information for that wide range of stakeholders.

We will examine this subject in some detail, discussing accounting fundamentals, the various areas where accounting professionals work and the information they produce. We will also examine the measures and ratios that accountants use to analyze an organization's performance and the important relationship between time and money. The fact that information is the product of accounting will remain foremost in this book.

Chapter 1 - Accounting is Different From Bookkeeping

Accounting is not bookkeeping. Bookkeeping concentrates on recording the organization's financial activities, whatever the business in which they are engaged. Maybe that is retail sales, home construction or manufacturing. No matter what business activity is taking place, someone must keep track of the transactions; selling, buying, repairing equipment, everything of significance. And in fact, even individuals must learn about accounting and must do certain bookkeeping tasks for their own personal finances, like balancing their checkbook and establishing personal budgets.

If the business is engaged in retail sales, bookkeepers record every sale, every purchase of inventory and every employee's pay. That is bookkeeping.

Accountants take this information and analyze, summarize and report the results. Remember, the product of accounting is information. This information is vital to management for their operating and investment decisions. Management must know how much money the business has, how much inventory it holds, how many employees are retained and how much they are being paid.

The viewpoint of a bookkeeper is the details. The viewpoint of an accountant is much broader and at a higher level. The accountant must be able to advise management on many decisions; how many more employees can be hired, what taxes are due and how to minimize them, analyzing investment decisions, and so forth.

Let's look at an example. Riverside Machine Company is a small manufacturer of components for the automobile industry. Their clients include almost all of the automobile manufacturers, and they are very busy when the industry is thriving.

The owners of Riverside are concerned about reducing manufacturing costs for a certain type of part that requires a lot of machining on several different types of machines. The engineers have determined that they can increase the rate of production by installing robots to load and unload the machines and transfer parts between them. The company has several robotic systems in operation now and is confident of their ability to incorporate these new robots. Currently, there is a serious backlog of work for these machines and improving the workflow would allow faster delivery with less overtime and not needing to work weekends to maintain production.

The engineers have determined all the necessary information related to this investment in terms of robot costs, tools needed by the robots, increases in production rate and effect on delivery time. They then sit down with the accounting experts to compute the improvements in cost, reductions in labor costs, shortening of delivery time and so forth. The accountant then uses all of this information to compute the effects on the firm's financial performance and profitability.

In most companies, the accountants compute a value for "Internal Rate of Return" for decisions by management. This rate of return serves as a threshold for new projects. It becomes one of the considerations used by management to decide whether or not to make the investment, in this case, in the new robots. Other considerations of course include delivery improvements, customer satisfaction, product quality and several others. That is a proper role for the accountant working with the engineers.

In addition to being a source of reliable financial information on these kinds of decisions, the accounting department also acts as what can be described as a "Scorekeeper", by monitoring costs and revenues, leading to profitability for the firm. This information is reported to management on a regular basis to help guide ongoing management decisions. The accountants cannot do much at all to influence the profitability of the firm directly, but their role is to report findings to management for them to make decisions.

The accounting function also leads the efforts at budgeting and budget reporting. These are more examples of the accounting product of information. These reports are available in varying levels of detail for publically owned companies and non-profit organizations. Privately owned companies are not required to publish these reports, except for those required by the government, regulatory and taxing authorities.

In their role as providers of information, they are often called upon for informed recommendations to help management decision making.

Chapter 2 - Understanding the Vocabulary

Every special area of interest has its own vocabulary, and accounting is the same. Many of the words used will be familiar to the reader but may have certain shades of meaning that are important. We need to understand this vocabulary. Here are some key definitions that are important to the accounting function.

Asset: an asset is anything the organization owns that helps it accomplish its mission. For a fast food restaurant, the grill or stove in the kitchen area is an asset. For a retail store, the inventory in the back room is an asset, along with display cases and shelves.

Liability: a liability is anything the organization owes to someone else. Unpaid wages to employees is a liability, taxes owed to the local government is a liability, unpaid insurance premiums for employee healthcare policies is a liability, bills for inventory that have not been paid is a liability.

Equity: equity is a measure of the claim of someone on the assets of the organization, such as liabilities (claims by the person or entity to whom the liability is owed, such as loans from a bank) and the investment by the owners of the organization.

Income: money flowing into the organization from its operations in whatever the line of business might be, for example, sales in a fast food restaurant, or rent collected on property the business owns.

Expense: this is the amount of money the organization needs to spend in order to carry out its operations. This represents payments to asset and service providers. For example, payments to a supplier of inventory items for a retail store.

Distributions: outflows of money to owners or stockholders, or bonuses to employees at the end of the year, for example.

Cash Flow: the term cash flow represents the money flowing through the operation, essentially income minus expenses. You can imagine a stream of money flowing into the organization with small streams going out as distributaries to pay for liabilities. The flow that is moving through this stream is the cash flow. How much is left at the end of the process is the profit for the firm.

Overhead: this is a group of costs not directly associated with the major function of the organization but necessary in order to make the organization accomplish its goals. For example, in a hospital, the janitorial staff that cleans and sanitizes the buildings, rooms and equipment are not directly associated with the hospital's patients, but they are absolutely essential. The labor and other costs like cleaning and sanitizing supplies are part of the organization's overhead. All the other myriad of costs like electricity, lighting, lawn maintenance, and even sweeping the parking lot are essential but not directly tied to the patients and their care. The accounting office is considered overhead for any organization not involved in the Public Accounting business.

GAAP: This is the term used to describe the Generally Accepted Accounting Principles. This is a set of 'rules' for the accounting profession, which must be followed to assure an accurate description of the financial activities of the organization. GAAP applies to all organizations that function in commerce, public service, and all other sectors of the general economy. Following these GAAP rules assures the public, the stockholders, the donors to non-profit organizations, the owners, employees and the taxing and regulatory authorities that the accounting for the organization is done in accordance with the proper methods and systems.

Each country establishes its own accounting standards but there exists an International Accounting Standards Board responsible for establishing and accrediting accounting standards for all nations who subscribe. Similarly, many countries establish similar Boards, to promulgate and enforce standards through certification and audit systems. These are in the form of standards, conventions and rules. Companies are not necessarily required to follow them but any publicly traded company must conform to the established Accounting Practices.

Chapter 3 – Accounting Reports: The Income Statement

Remember that the product of accounting is information. The three most common forms for that information are the "Income Statement", the "Balance Sheet", and the "Cash Flow Statement." Every organization uses some form of these three documents and usually all three. We will explore the Balance Sheet in Chapter 4 and the Cash Flow Statement in Chapter 5.

The Income Statement or Profit and Loss Statement (or P&L statement) can be imagined as a video tape of the organization over some period of time, like a month, six months or a year. This statement tells management how the firm is doing from the standpoint of "Are we making money or not?" Of course, this is a very fundamental question, since after a number of periods of losses, the firm will no longer be viable and will go out of business.

The most important use of the Income Statement is to compare it with prior periods and with the period budget. If management has determined that the firm must meet certain performance levels, they need the answer to the question above; "How are we doing compared with our goals and budget?" Each organization has an established and agreed upon budget. The budget contains allocations of resources for all of the activities of the organization, from sales, purchases of materials for sale or production, employee salaries and benefits and even overhead items like electricity and water.

These budgets are set up, usually each year, to guide the managers and supervisors in what decisions can be made to commit resources like money and labour, and for what purposes. Based on this budget, which has been agreed upon by management, it acts as a steering mechanism for the firm's operations. The periodic P&L reports represent the

Accounting function's role in keeping score. Here is an example of a P&L Statement or an Income Statement. We will look at each of these entries to see what they represent, based on The Martin Company.

THE MARTIN COMPANY, INC.
INCOME STATEMENT
(FIRST HALF, 2014)
JANUARY 1, 2014 THROUGH JUNE 30, 2014
(all amounts in thousands of dollars)

Sales, Gross: $116,410
Less: Returns and Allowances: $3,075
Net Sales: $113,335

Less Cost of Goods Sold: $78,683
Less Current Depreciation Charges: $1,450
Gross Profit: $33,202

Operating Expenses
Selling and Promotion: $18,005
General and Administration: $8,910
Total Operating Expenses: $26,915

Operating Profit: $6,287
(Gross Profit minus Operating Expense)

Other Income and Expense
Interest and Dividend Income: $363
less: Interest Expense: $917
Net Interest Expense: $554
Profit Before Taxes: $5,733
Taxes on Income at 35%: $2,007
Net Profit: $3,726

This P&L or Income Statement is for the Martin Company. The Martin Company manufacturers small household appliances, which are sold through distributors under Martin's label and major discount and department stores under their labels. Manufacturing operations are located in a small town in the Midwest. The key technologies employed by the firm include manufacturing of fractional horsepower motors, injection molding of plastic parts and machining of miscellaneous small metal parts such as shafts, armatures and gears as well as assembly of the products, packaging and shipping them to customers.

As it says at the top, this report covers the first half of the year. For this company, their budget year is a calendar year. Some organizations may use other budget years. Government organizations often use October 1 through September 30 as a budget year. A mid-year report is very valuable to management, to keep track of performance, especially in complex organizations.

Total Sales; The first line entered is the total sales for that period. This is the value of products shipped to customers. In some cases, there may be returns from customers for any number of reasons; wrong color, wrong address, quality issues, and so forth. This is recorded as Returns and Allowances and is subtracted from Gross Sales resulting in Net Sales.

Cost of Goods Sold; The line labeled Cost of Goods Sold represents the cost that Martin incurred in producing the products shipped during that period. That will include the materials and components purchased, the labor used to produce these products and may include machine time if that is the procedure for Martin Company.

Depreciation; Martin Company must also account for the wear and tear on their productive assets ranging from big, expensive plastic injection molding machines to company vehicles. This is a real cost that must be accounted for but is not a cash expense. It is determined by the accounting office and along with the

Cost of Goods Sold, reduces the net sales to give the amount of Gross Profit. This loss of value of assets is called depreciation and is subtracted from sales, even though it is not a cash expense. Depreciation will be covered in a later section.

Operating Expenses; However, this is not the complete picture of costs incurred. The items labeled Operating Expenses include the salaries of the supervisors, managers, sales representatives, shipping operators, energy costs like electric power and gas, office expenses for papers, copiers, and the myriad of other costs necessary to produce the products that generate sales income. In some companies, this lump of costs may be referred to as "Overhead." Overhead is a necessary expense and must be included in the budget and in P&L statement. Managers and supervisors work hard to keep Overhead costs to a minimum. Overhead also includes taxes paid on the real estate and other ad valorum taxes. These amounts are shown as Selling and Promotion as well as

General and Administrative or G&A. G&A usually includes the Overhead costs.

Operating Profit; After accounting for the Operating Expenses, we are left with the Operating Profit. Operating Profit is the first measure of how effective Martin Company is in carrying out its main objective, making and selling products. Operating Profit is the Gross Profit minus the Operating Expenses.

Other Income and Expense; But, Martin Company must also take into account the other costs such as interest on loans they need to purchase equipment and materials. They may have other incidental income from sources like investments, rental property receipts and royalties. These are all included in the P&L statement but are not part of the major business, making and selling products.

Profit Before Taxes; When all of that is included, we see the Profit Before Taxes or PBT. That profit must be reduced by the taxes paid on the sales and other income, and we finally get to see the profits resulting from the major business of

Martin. This is what managers call the "Bottom Line."

Managers and supervisors are vitally concerned with how the P&L Statement compares with the budget and how it is changing over time. Are we earning more profit this year than we did in the same period last year and in prior years? Continual growth in profit makes it possible of Martin to stay in business, producing products, serving customers and employing people. It is also essential to being able to expand the business, adding more products and investing in advanced technologies that customers demand.

Chapter 4 - The Balance Sheet

A short description of the Balance Sheet is that it states "What we own and what we owe." Think of the Balance Sheet as a photograph of the business at a point in time. Just as the Income Statement is a recording of progress over time, the Balance Sheet gives us a picture of the company at some requested time, say at the end of the year or mid-year as shown here for the Martin Company. The Balance Sheet may also be called the Position Statement.

THE MARTIN COMPANY, INC.
BALANCE SHEET
AS OF JUNE 30, 2014
Assets in $,000's,
Current Assets
Cash: $2,493
Accounts Receivable: $18,610
Inventory: $9,308
Prepaids: $780
Total Current Assets:$31,191
Long Term Assets

Investments: $7,300
Property and Equipment: $22,730
Less Accumulated Depreciation ($7,382)
Intangibles: $2,670
Total Long Term Assets: $29,044
Total Assets: $60,235

LIABILITIES AND OWNER'S EQUITY, in $,000's

Current Liabilities
Accounts Payable: $5,350
Salaries and Benefits Payable: $2,480
Taxes Payable: $1,855
Notes Payable within 1 year: $5,000
Total Current Liabilities: $14,685
Long Term Debt: $15,000
Owner's Equity
Invested Capital: $15,000
Retained Earnings: $15,550
Total Owner's Equity: $30,550
Total Liabilities and Owner's Equity: $60,235

We will describe each of these line items in the order shown on the Balance Sheet. Just as with the Income Statement, all these figures are shown in thousands.

Assets are "What we Own"

Current Items

Current Assets; those assets which we can access quickly, such as 90 days.

Cash; represents money in demand deposits, like a checking account, needed for paying current bills like utilities and wages. A company's cash may also be held in short term investments like Certificates of Deposit with maturity dates of one year or less.

Accounts Receivable; the money we have billed to customers but have not yet received. If we receive a check in the mail today paying an invoice for products shipped, the amount in the Accounts Receivable will be decreased by that amount and the Cash Account will be increased by the same amount.

Inventory; represents all the finished goods that have been produced and are awaiting shipment, along with all of the material that is currently being worked on and all of the raw materials on hand. Other items like processing materials and maintenance supplies, office supplies and so forth are included here.

Prepaids; is another interesting account. When Martin Company paid the property taxes for this year, say in January that is called a prepaid, since that expense will last for the entire year. Insurance premiums, investments in retirement plans and so forth are usually included as prepaids.

The amount of current assets for Martin Company, $31,191, is the total for current assets.

Long Term Items

Long Term Assets are the fixed assets that will last for many accounting periods. For instance, if Martin has purchased an interest in another company, that represents an investment. Similarly, stocks, bonds and other financial instruments are categorized as investments. These are non-depreciable assets. We will cover depreciation next, under Property and Equipment

Property and Equipment; the value of all the land, buildings, warehouses, machinery used in production and all the other equipment that has been purchased in the past and is or could be used in production, shipping and sales of Martin Company's products. However, all of this reflects past purchases, and except for land but including buildings, has a finite lifetime. A plastic injection-molding machine, bought new four years ago, will no longer be valuable at some time in the future. The loss in value can be due to wear and tear and even technological obsolescence. When it loses all its value, it will be taken out of production and perhaps sold for its scrap value. This decrease in value is recognized through the accounting process called depreciation.

Essentially all assets in the company are continuously losing value, either through wear out, age or technological advances. For instance, the computer system used to track production is, like all other computer and high technology assets, becoming obsolete continuously. Assets are being consumed by time, technology or wear. The building for example, has a finite lifetime. At some point, Martin Company will need to replace the building or at least make a major refurbishment, just because of its age. If no new long-term assets are purchased, the value of the total Property and Equipment line will decrease each period to reflect depreciation.

Depreciation: The costs for depreciation are actual costs in that they reflect the diminishment in value of an asset through its use or age. These depreciation costs are not actual cash costs, that is, they do not represent funds flowing out of the firm but they are necessary costs incurred in order to produce products or services. These depreciation charges are generally included in a separate line in the P&L Statement, as shown above.

The methods used for allocating the cost of an asset over its lifetime, that is depreciation are beyond the scope of this book. However, the methods used are frequently set by the taxing authority, since it reduces the profit before taxes and hence, the amount of tax paid. It also affects any ad valorem taxes on property and equipment.

Intangibles; is a general category for all the other assets of the firm such as royalties on patents held by the company, trademarks, copyrights, organization costs, and more. These Intangible Assets may have infinite lifetime, with respect to the existence of the company, and are usually not subject to depreciation.

The total of Current and Long term Assets gives the total asset value of the firm. For our example of Martin Company, this amounts to about 60 million dollars, ($60,235,000). This number will appear again in the other side of the Balance Sheet where the liabilities are shown. Remember that the Balance Sheet shows what we own and what we owe. The liabilities are what we owe. We can also think of Liabilities as the source of the capital we have invested to purchase land, buildings, equipment, inventory and the like, our assets.

Liabilities - "What we Owe"

What we owe is funds owed to someone outside the firm or to the owners of the firm. These are all called liabilities because sooner or later, they must be paid.

Current Liabilities Current Liabilities are those which must be paid within a year or less. Accounts payable are the bills we have received but not yet paid, for anything we have purchased. Raw materials, purchased parts, shipping invoices, office supplies, lease payments for things like a copy machine, all fall under the umbrella of Current Liabilities.

Salaries and Benefits Payable; are just that. We do not pay employees every day. We must show on the balance sheet the amounts that have been accrued and will be paid in the next payment cycle. Outstanding invoices for things like employee medical and life insurance, workers compensation insurance premiums and salaries for supervisors and executives are all included in Salaries and Benefits Payable. Clearly, these fit the description of what we owe.

Taxes; may be accrued and this line represents the acknowledgment of this debt. Taxes may be income taxes for the firm, employee withholding taxes for social security or employee income tax, local taxes including property and ad valorem taxes and so forth. This is a debt that must be paid.

Notes Payable within 1 year; represents any short term borrowing Martin Company may have done for whatever purpose and is due within the next twelve months. For example, a company may choose to borrow funds to finance an increase in inventory. These are short-term notes.

The sum of these is the total of Current Liabilities. Most companies borrow some amounts of money to pay for things like raw materials inventory in anticipation of a seasonal or cyclical increase in sales.

Long Term Debt is for things like bonds we may have sold to raise capital, bank or other financing company loans due beyond the next year. Long Term Debt and Current Liabilities is the amount the firm owes to entities outside of the firm.

Invested Capital; is the money the owners contributed in order to start the firm and if, at any point since, the owners have invested more money to expand or maintain the business. This may have taken place a number of years ago or may be invested periodically, as the owners choose to put more money into the business.

Retained Earnings; is not cash in the bank. It is the value of the firm built up during its years of existence. It represents the money not distributed to owners or spent to maintain operations, like buying raw material. It is the profits retained and used to buy assets like property and equipment, invest in long term assets such as production equipment, buildings and parking lots.

The total of Invested Capital and Retained Earnings represents the owners' share of the business. For Martin Company, the total is $60,235,000. Notice that this is exactly equal to the total assets shown above. The fact that these two numbers are equal is not an accident. This equality is why this report is called the Balance Sheet. It shows the balance between what we own and what we owe. Chapter 6 will discuss that balance further, as the Accounting Equation.

Chapter 5 – The Cash Flow Statement

Every organization depends on its immediate cash reserves to pay its bills. This is not different from a personal household, where the householder must keep money in a savings or checking account to pay all the bills that are due. On some occasions, the individual may choose to keep cash but that is not recommended because of the risk of loss or theft. Companies and organizations do not pay in cash for the same reasons.

What is important to any organization or individual is that there is sufficient money flowing into the cash account to cover current liabilities. The flow of money into and out of the organization is called its Cash Flow, and is reported on the Cash Flow Statement.

For private and public owned firms, for-profit companies, the primary source of revenue is the firm's operations. Whether it is in the manufacturing, retailing, servicing or any other sector, its operations are the reason the firm exists. For non-profits and charitable organizations, the main income is from donations and fund raising. That is their operations equivalent.

There are usually three streams of cash flow reported, if the organization is involved in all three. They are:

1) Cash flow from operations

2) Cash flow from investments

3) Cash flow from financing activities

Cash Flow from Operations
Operations cash flow is just that; cash flowing into and out of the operations of the organization. The cash flow statements are taken directly from the Income Statement and the Balance Sheet. We will use Martin Company as our example. Many organizations have different rules for determining cash flow.

For Martin, remember their Income Statement showed cash at $2,493,000 shown in thousands as $2,493. There are several other lines for which we must account. Accountants base the cash flow statement Operating Profit, PBT or Profit Before taxes. The cash shown is part of that PBT, at $5,733.

Martin has incurred depreciation charges but these are not cash expenditures so they must be added back into the cash flow. Receivables are also liquid assets and represent cash flow in the near future.

Inventories represent cash already spent or committed so they do not add to cash flow, at least not until they are used in operations and sold as products. However, some firms may include inventory in cash flow. That is determined by the organization.

Similarly, accounts payable and any other accrued liabilities must also be subtracted from net income since they are liabilities that must be paid with cash. These might be salaries and wages due at the end of the period.

The final amount represents the Net Cash Flow from Operations for Martin Company for that period. The accountants then compare that with the same cash flow from the previous period to see if cash is increasing or decreasing. Organizations always want the cash flow to increase, since that represents their ability to meet their obligations, pay the owners and lenders and certainly, to grow the business by expansion.

Cash Flow from Investing

However, this is not the only user of cash. The company must pay for any assets it purchases during the period or funds used to pay for assets previously purchased. This is the Cash Flow From Investing, in this case, investing in plant and equipment. Any capital assets acquired during this period must be shown in this line item.

In the case of The Martin Company, no new assets were acquired during this period so that entry is zero.

Cash Flow from Financing Activities

The company must also meet its long-term liabilities which may be in the form of long-term notes it has issued in the past and must be repaid. For a publicly owned organization, any dividends also consume cash and they appear under financing activities, since selling stock is a means to finance the company. In the same way, for privately held organizations, any payments to the owners are made from cash so they must be included in the cash flow statement.

Cash Flow Statement The Martin Company
January 1, 2014 through June 30, 2014
(All amounts in thousands of dollars)

Cash Flow from Operations	($000's dollars
Operating Profit	6,287
Depreciation	1,450
Accounts Receivable	18,610
Inventory	(9,308)
Accounts Payable	(5,350)
Salaries and Benefits Payable	(2,480)
Taxes Payable	(1,855)
Net Cash Flow from Operations	**7,354**
Cash Flow from Investing	
None for this period	
Cash Flow from Financing Activities	
Interest and Dividend Income	363
Interest Expense	(917)
Net Interest Expense	(554)
Net Cash from Financing Activities	(554)

Total Cash Flow at End of Period	**6,800**

Chapter 6 – The Accounting Equation

The Accounting Equation is probably the most fundamental part of accounting as it is done in modern times. It captures the concept described in the Balance Sheet. That concept is that for any going concern, what the concern owns comes from only two sources, funds borrowed, expressed as liabilities and funds owed to the owners, their equity.

Assets = Liabilities + Owner's Equity
This equation is often expressed in its expanded form;

Assets = Liabilities+ Owner's Capital+ Revenues- Expenses- Owner Draws
In this form, it describes more of the operations of the firm. The assets of the firm come from:

Liabilities; money contributed by entities outside the firm such as long term and short term loans from banks or investment companies, sale of stock, bonds sold, and so forth.

Owner's Capital; the funds supplied by the owners and the profits generated by the operations.

Shareholder Stock; owners can be shareholders of common or preferred stocks, frequently sold on a stock exchange

Revenues; money generated by the operations of the firm and other sources of revenue or income

Expenses; costs incurred in the operation of the firm such as material, labor and all the other expenses

Owner Draws; money withdrawn from the company and paid to the owners, as profits withdrawn, dividends, bonuses or in any other form.

One can see that the expanded version better describes the operation of the firm in carrying out its business, whether that business is retail sales, manufacturing, mining, or any other activity designed to generate revenues and profits. Even hospitals and other service businesses follow this same expanded model.

Revenues are generated, expenses incurred and paid, and profits distributed. Of course, this appears very much different for all of the various business models under which firms operate. This expanded equation describes the business models for large, international firms that are publicly owned by stockholders, all the way down to the small privately owned construction firms, farms or service business owned and operated by self-employed entrepreneurs. Every organization can be seen to operate exactly by this accounting equation.

For example, Riverside Machine Company, illustrated in Chapter 1, The Martin Company illustrated in Chapters 3, 4 and 5 and all the other firms in whatever businesses one can imagine, all follow this universal accounting equation. It truly is universal in its application, for companies and organizations of all sizes, in all industries, in all countries in the world. This is truly the fundamental equation of accounting.

And, all accounting and accountants, in all these businesses must follow the earlier discussed GAAP, generally accepted accounting principles establish by authorities and certification bodies.

Banks, investment firms, investment fund managers, and everyone else in all market sectors are subject to this universal fundamental equation. We will see this in the subsequent chapters as we describe the various accounting professionals, their functions and responsibilities in all aspects of the accounting world.

Chapter 7 – The CPA and Public Accounting

Probably the most recognized accounting professionals are the CPAs, the Certified Public Accountants. These professionals may work for very large accounting firms like PriceWaterhouseCoopers® or KPMG®, two internationally known and respected accounting firms with offices in most countries around the world or the small one or two person offices in almost every city and town in every nation. CPAs perform many valuable services for all types of businesses and organizations. A church, for example, must file and pay the required payroll taxes for all employees on a timely basis. CPAs can set up the accounting systems for a church secretary or bookkeeper to use in meeting these requirements.

Similarly, any organization must establish responsibility and authority for internal auditing. Auditing in general means that the organization must carry out the accounting function in accordance with established standards and must assure management that the records are being kept accurately and in compliance with these standards and laws. This internal auditing function is normally carried out by employees of the organization who are educated, trained and hired for that purpose, usually within the organization's financial control office. This internal auditing task may also be outsourced to an independent firm such as a CPA company.

External auditing is required by law for all publicly owned companies and other organizations. External auditing must be carried out by a qualified external authority, who is not part of the organization being audited. CPA's can serve as these Independent External Auditors. They must represent an independent third party, a role most often carried out by an organization in business as CPAs or External Auditors. These can be small, individual business firms or large multinational companies, like those mentioned above and many more.

For publicly owned companies, that is firms who sell stock certificates, privately or through a stock market, the external audit report is extremely important and is addressed to the stockholders. For privately held firms, the report is addressed to the owners and the highest level of management. Shareholders rely on the external audit report to assure them that the firm is carrying out its accounting for the business activities in accordance with the GAAP or other applicable standards.

For non-profits and charitable organizations, the report is addressed to the Board of Directors.

Sharon Haas for example, is a graduate of a mid-western university with a degree in Business Administration where she majored in accounting and an MBA with a focus on Accounting and Finance. She has ten years experience in accounting for a medium sized manufacturing firm in

Chicago, Illinois. The State of Illinois as most other states in the US requires 150 hours of education to qualify for the CPA certificate and license. The MBA is frequently used to meet this requirement. Many states also have a requirement for continuing education to maintain the CPA license. Sharon passed the required examination and was issued her license after her graduate studies.

At present, she works as an external auditor for one of the multinational CPA firms, in their office in Cleveland, Ohio. Her client assignments are a number of firms in Ohio, Michigan, Wisconsin and Illinois. She is a member of AICPA, the American Institute of CPAs.

As an external auditor, she maintains a relationship with her client firms, providing consultant services in the areas of taxes, investments, capital purchases and accounting. Every year, she visits each client firm to carry out her external audit duties. She has an assistant who travels with her, helping in the audit duties and in preparing the annual audit report.

Sharon enjoys her work with both her employer and her clients. She says there is never a dull day; every day brings on new questions and different challenges.

One of the most important responsibilities that Sharon and all other external auditors have is to be careful with is to maintain the position of an objective outside authority. Sharon, like most professionals, is friendly and outgoing but she has to be careful that she separates her feelings from her work. She must be objective and dispassionate while doing her work. She must maintain an 'arm's length' attitude toward her clients. She must maintain her professional standards and report based on what she finds, not what her client may say. Stories abound of auditing firms, some with very famous names who did not maintain this objectivity and sense of responsibility to the stockholders and stakeholders in carrying out their functions as an objective external auditor. Sharon's reputation and her license depend on her professional attitude.

Chapter 8 – Jobs in Accounting: Financial Accounting

Most organizations and business firms have someone in charge of the financial office. Frequently this is called the Comptroller's Office (pronounced controller) and is staffed with people educated and trained in accounting. The head of the office is frequently a CPA and directs the staff in her office as well as providing advice and counsel to the top management. This position is usually one that reports directly to the owner or owners of the firm, or to the CEO (Chief Executive Officer) and is often referred to as the CFO or Chief Financial Officer.

In the private sector, these jobs are usually challenging and of course, vital to the health of the operation. One such member of management is George Wilson. He is the CFO for a medium sized firm,

Catch of the Day Restaurants, a chain of restaurants, specializing in seafood meals.

George is the head of comptrollers office and reports on the firm's financial position. He uses several important indicators, in addition to the periodic income statements. Balance sheets are updated annually since they tend to change more slowly than other reports. Here are two of the important measures, expressed as ratios.

Current Ratio is a comparison of how well the firm is prepared to meet its current obligations, and is expressed as the ratio of current assets to current liabilities.

Current Ratio

Current Assets/Current Liabilities

If an organization finds itself with a current ratio of less than unity, that means it is at risk of being illiquid to the extent that it may become bankrupt. It does not have the means to pay its current obligations. These may be payables to suppliers, wages and salaries to employees or taxes due to the government. None of these can be sustained for long periods of time.

The firm's accountants may suggest strategies such as taking on long term debt to reduce current short term debt by means of paying off important payables but there is likely to be a serious underlying problems that is causing the organization to not be able to generate revenue with its assets.

If we look back at the Income Statement for Martin Company, we can see that the Current Ratio is $31,191/$14,685 or 2.13. This indicates Martin Company has more than enough current assets to meet its current liabilities, even if it encounters difficulties in generating revenue for a short period of time.

An example of a situation in which a firm might find jeopardy is the event of a serious business interruption like a flood or fire. The liabilities will not go away just because the firm cannot operate but the current assets will shrink rapidly since there will be no revenue for a period of time. If the firm is able to get back into operation quickly, they might avert disaster. This is an instance when business interruption insurance may be a strong recommendation by the accounting department.

Another important ratio measures the efficiency of the firm, that is, how well is it doing in converting its resources into revenue and is calculated by the ratio between Operating Expenses and Operating Revenue, both of which come from the Income Statement. This is called the Operating Ratio.

Operating Ratio

Operating Expenses/Operating Revenue

For the Martin Company, the Operating Ratio is $26,915/$34,652 or 0.78. This number must always be less than 1 and the smaller, the better. There are two important ways to analyze this number. First, is the current level compared with the prior periods? The second is to compare, wherever possible, to similar ratios for other companies in the same industry. As standalone ratios, they do not mean much. However, for example, when the Operating Ratio gets close to 1.0 or even exceeds 1.0, the firm is in serious trouble because its operating expenses exceed its operating revenue. The Current Ratio should always be greater than 1.0, meaning that the firm can meet its current obligations and the Operating Ratio must be significantly less than 1.

George makes certain that these numbers are accurate and in fact, since Catch of the Day maintains an internal local area network for its managers, he posts these numbers on the internal system and because his software closes out each day, the top management can see these important ratios almost on a Real Time basis.

Remember that the product of accounting is information and information is valuable to management only when it is available, timely, dependable and accurate.

We will discuss these and many more indicators and ratios in a later chapter.

Chapter 9 – Tax Accounting

Almost all countries have complex tax systems, covering the range from income taxes, property taxes, tariffs on imported goods, sales taxes, value added taxes, and anything else that the governments can think of. The watchword might be "if it moves, tax it, if it doesn't move, tax it anyway." These systems can be very complex and taxes are applied at all levels of government. One of the most important services accountants perform is keeping track of the client's tax liability and making certain it is paid, on time and in the right amount.

These specialists are in demand in all countries and all industries. Not understanding and complying with the myriad tax laws can get an organization in trouble faster than almost anything else and it requires a specialist to make sure the right taxes are paid and that the client does not pay more tax than is required by law.

Tax accountants work in large and small firms, and can even be on staff for large, complex multinational CPA and Consulting organizations. Many other tax accountants are self-employed and also serve other accounting tasks for a variety of clients. Carl Waters is such a tax accountant. He operates a small accounting firm in a medium sized city in Indiana. Carl employs three people, all of whom are trained in accounting and Carl himself is a CPA.

Carl spent 12 years working for the IRS as a tax agent and then became an Enrolled Agent before he opened his own office. Enrolled Agents are certified by the IRS as qualified to advise clients on tax matters and to represent them before the IRS authorities. Because of his years with the IRS, Carl is very familiar with many industries. He decided to open his own office six years ago and has an important list of clients. He and his staff perform many accounting functions for these clients in addition to preparing tax returns and setting up the recording systems needed within the client firm to maintain the records required. He also advises clients on ways to reduce their tax liability, within the limits of the tax laws.

Chapter 10 – Accounting Consultants

Many organizations, especially large firms have a myriad of issues with which accountants must deal. Setting up accounting systems, assisting in public stock offerings, developing long-term strategic plans and so forth are tasks for which many organizations seek outside help from specialized consulting firms and many of these include large numbers of accountants.

Accountants working for these consulting firms often develop specific areas of expertise in which they provide skills that the requesting firms and organizations cannot afford to employ full time.

Many of these consulting firms offer a wide range of services including but certainly not limited to management services, marketing studies, investment counseling, stock offerings, fraud investigation (forensic accounting), human resources management and personnel development, taxes, international business matters and more.

Many of these organizations select certain industries or sectors as areas of specialization, such as aerospace and defense, automotive industries, medical management, chemical industries or public sector, to name a few.

Accountants who work in these organizations often find themselves with a variety of clients and develop specialties important to the firms. Not all of them must be accountants but in general, a study of accountancy is a common starting point.

Helen Crandall is just such an employee. She works for an internationally known consulting firm with offices in many countries. Helen's specialty in helping client firms "Go Public", that is to issue and sell stock in order to expand their funding and ownership. They may be changing from a privately held firm to one that is publicly owned.

Helen has undergraduate and graduate degrees in Law and is a member of the Bar Association in her state of Connecticut. After completing her law studies, she continued in school and earned an MBA. This qualified her to become a CPA and develop her specialty. Most of the dealings are with firms across the country but since she is so deeply involved in Wall Street, she has her office in New York City. In her work, she advises companies in how to make the change from private to public ownership.

Chapter 11 - Forensic Accounting

Harold Waterson is an FBI Agent working in the field of Forensic Accounting. He has a Bachelor's Degree in Accounting from a Midwestern state university and has completed a Master's Degree in Forensic Accounting from a well-known University. He has been with the FBI for 12 years, after completing the mandatory 20 weeks of training at the FBI facility in Quantico, Virginia. Prior to joining the FBI, he worked as an accountant for a major public accounting firm.

He works for the FBI as a Forensic Accountant, investigating a wide range of illicit activities ranging from public official corruption to money laundering and fraud. He is a CPA and belongs to the American Board of Forensic Accounting and the American Institute of CPAs.

In his job, he is required to travel all around the United States, investigating his wide range of issues. His favorite investigation involves corruption of public officials. To do so, he often has to interview the individuals involved, others in the official's office, people accused of offering bribes or whatever the specific case involves.

Harold feels very satisfied with his profession and his accomplishments. He knows that public corruption is present and causes losses to the general public and distorts the normal functioning of government.

In addition to the investigation part, he must also frequently testify in court when these suspects are tried for their crimes. Part of his FBI training helped him become comfortable in testifying as an expert witness.

Mary Kay Ryan is also a forensic accountant but she works for one of the major consulting firms. She has a Bachelor's degree in accounting and a Master's Degree in economics and she is a CPA. She belongs to the American Board of Forensic Accounting and the American Institute of CPAs.

Her job does not require nearly as much travel as others in her field and she seldom has to testify in court. Rather, she works in the corporate office in Cleveland, Ohio and spends her time reviewing records for clients who are worried about internal embezzling by employees, usually called "white collar crime".

She reports to the head of the Forensic Division of her firm and is responsible for reviewing evidence brought to her by the field agents. These agents are not necessarily forensic accountants and receive guidance from the team leader of the investigation in the field. Instead, she carefully examines the evidence and reports her findings to the team leader.

Chapter 12 - Personal Accounting

Everyone who has income and expenses needs to carry out Personal Accounting, ranging from balancing a checkbook to filing personal tax returns. These people do not have to be trained in bookkeeping or accounting but do need to keep certain records. This is part of Personal Accounting.

Other parts of personal accounting are things like keeping track of bills so they can be paid on time, establishing a budget and monitoring many other bits of information like credit card invoices, to watch for errors and unauthorized charges.

In today's atmosphere of Identity Theft, we all need to learn to work as a forensic accountant, analyzing what charges were made, by whom and working with the bank or credit card company to get these charges removed.

At other times, everyone must be tax accountants, taking action to minimize tax liabilities, keeping track of legitimate deductions and filing the return.

Chapter 13 – Measures and Ratios

The product of accounting is information. This chapter examines the form and determination of the important information accountants need to produce and report to management, owners, stakeholders and stockholders. The Comptroller's Office has the responsibility of setting up the recording, analysis and reporting structures to keep management informed of the condition of the organization, giving warnings and counsel to management in advance of issues to prevent adverse situations.

To do so, the CFO will use two types of strategies for extracting important information; static and dynamic. Static analysis measures various important signals at some point in time, for example, the current ration as described earlier. These are measures taken at some point in time, to assess the current situation. Dynamic analyses are those that examine the organization's performance over some period of time, like month-to-month or year over year. These dynamic analyses provide important trend analysis, allowing some prediction of future performance under these same conditions. That means 'here is what will be in the future if we don't make a change.'

These measures are taken from both the Balance Sheet and from the Income Statement, depending upon the model needed. These measures can be grouped into three categories; measures of financial strength, operating efficiency and organization profitability. See Appendix 1 for illustrations of many of these measures and ratios.

Financial Strength
Long Term Financial Strength:

An organization must be able to withstand the normal and sometimes worse than normal vicissitudes of its life. It must be in a position of strength to maintain its ability to carry out its chosen mission, whether that mission is manufacturing, extraction, service or distribution. The many stakeholders and stockholders expect that management will be capable of guiding the firm through the perils of everyday business life without failing or going out of business. The organization must be resilient and able to maintain its forward progress under any reasonably expected events.

Here are some commonly used measures of financial strength:

Equity to Liabilities Ratio:

$$\frac{\text{Owner's Equity}}{\text{Total Liabilities}}$$

Remember that all assets of the organization must come from either inside the operation or by borrowing from outside. This ratio shows the source of the assets as a proportion from the Owner's Equity and from all Liabilities, including Current Liabilities. In modern terms, "How much skin do the owners have in the game?" A low ratio indicates that most of the assets come from outside the organization, not from the owners. A higher ratio, approaching unity would indicate a solidly built firm with good grounding by the owners. Too low a ratio might indicate high levels of borrowing or high levels of current liabilities. Too high a ratio might indicate the opportunity to leverage the assets by increasing outside funding from sources such as long-term loans or bonds.

Times Interest Earned:

Net Income Before Interest and Taxes/Total Interest Payments

Whatever leverage strategy the organization chooses, it must pay the interest on outstanding loans, both short term and long term. The holders of this debt want assurance that the organization can earn enough to pay the interest owed on a timely basis. This ratio captures that ability. A low number indicates risk for the lenders, a higher number of times interest earned is an indication of safety.

Debt to Equity Ratio:

The Debt to Equity Ratio measures the degree to which the organization is leveraged, between assets and debt. This is particularly informative for long-term debt, since short-term debt like accounts payable is usually very fluid and is not a useful source of operating capital.

> **Total Debt (Current and Long Term)/Total Equity**

Together, these three ratios can show the strength of the firm in terms of its ability to meet its obligations and the extent to which the owners have contributed to that strength.

Short Term Financial Strength:
Current Ratio:

As described earlier, the Current Ratio tells us how well the firm is prepared to meet its current obligations, and is expressed as the ratio of current assets to current liabilities.

> **Current Assets/Current Liabilities**

This ratio is one with two edges; a larger number indicates good assurance of meeting current liabilities, i.e. the organization is very capable of meeting its short-term obligations. However, too large a ratio might indicate that current assets, like cash and cash equivalents are being held in preference to being put to work earning profits.

Quick Ratio:

The Quick Ratio is a bit more severe than the Current Ratio because is compares only the total of cash and accounts receivable with current liabilities. This leaves out the value of the inventory and prepaids and is regarded as a better assessment of strength in the immediate sense. This ratio is sometimes called the Acid Test. It does represent the availability if immediate action to resolve Current Liabilities is needed.

$$(Cash + AccountsReceivable)$$
$$/Current\ Liabilities$$

Operating Efficiency

Measures of Operating Efficiency tell management how well and effectively they are using the assets they have. These are easy calculations but are very useful as a static measure and for watching trends over time as dynamic analyses.

Receivables Turnover:

The Receivables Turnover Ratio indicates how efficient the organization is at collecting money due from customers. Like the others, this is an easy calculation and these results should be available at request from the accounting system. This ratio should be as low as possible, indicating prompt payment by customers.

Net Sales/ Average Accounts Receivable

Inventory Turnover:

Inventory is an asset in which the organization has chosen to invest. In practice, investments in inventory represent opportunities lost to invest in more productive assets and should be minimized with a well-planned material control system. Keeping track of Inventory Turnover is important for an operation trying to apply concepts of Lean Management.

> **Cost of Goods Sold/Average Inventory**

Turnover of Assets:

Like receivables and inventory, assets are investment choices by the organization's management. This measure is not too common but is informative. It shows how well the management is employing the assets is holds. It reveals how many times the total assets are being used in the firm's operation.

> **Total Sales/Average Total Assets**

Operating Ratio:

The operating ratio shows how much of each unit of revenue is consumed by operating expense, and how much is left over to contribute to the firm's profits.

> **Operating Expense/Operating Revenue**

Profitability

One of the most important indicators for management and outside stakeholders are the measures of profitability.

Profit Margin:

This may be the most recognized measure of the profitability of the organization and is a widely used measure. It is usually expressed as a percentage. This is often referred to as Return on Sales or ROS.

It is frequently used in one of two forms, the second being a little more restrictive in that it eliminates any revenue from sources other than operations.

> **Net Income/Total Revenues**
> **Net Operating Income/Total Sales**

Return on Investment:

Return on Investment or ROI or Return on Assets (ROA) is another very commonly used measure of the profitability of a firm. The individual accounting analyst may choose whether to use Average Total

Assets and Net Income Before Taxes and Interest or some other shading that may suit the needs of the firm better. For example, the analyst may choose to exclude other income such as interest, rents and royalties and restrict this measure only to operations.

> **Net Income Before Taxes and Interest/Total Assets**

Return on Equity:

A similar measure examines the equity of the owners, for a privately held organization, total owner's equity or for a publicly held organization, total stock equity. Again, the details should be left to the management as to exactly how to compute Return on Equity or ROE.

> **Net Income Before Taxes and Interest/Total Equity**

Return on Capital Employed

This ratio, often called ROCE, measures how efficiently the firm uses its capital investment to earn profits. The ratio is shown below.

$$\frac{\text{Profit before Interest and Taxes}}{\text{Total Assets} - \text{Current Liabilities}}$$

Chapter 14 – Accounting Software

For all but the smallest organizations, accounting software is essential to an effective financial control system. Individuals selling items on the internet for example, may be able to keep the necessary records manually, in hard copy on paper or a computer spreadsheet, but the image of old time accountants sitting at a wooden desk wearing green eyeshades and working with an ink pen, is interesting history but today's world requires much better systems. Think of Charles Dickens' characters Ebenezer Scrooge and Bob Cratchet.

When an organization, whether for profit or not-for-profit, has more than one individual with responsibilities, a real accounting system is needed and the larger the organization, the greater the need for a computer based system.

The simplest of these may be ones like QuickBooks®, SAGE 50®, XERO® or WAVE®, useful for small to medium size businesses. An advantage of several of these is that no accounting training is needed to set them up and operate them. They all tend to be very intuitive.

Larger organizations needing more comprehensive accounting packages have a wide variety from which to select. These more complex systems usually require specialized training available from the software vendors.

A few characteristics are common to all packages. First, they should be designed with easy to use graphical interfaces, intuitive command structures and system design. They should be capable of producing the common accounting reports using the well-known ratios, percentages and rates common to all accounting systems. They should also be able to generate such reports on demand and to track progress of this information over time for trend analyses.

Many are adaptable to integrated data management ranging from order entry, invoicing, shipping data, inventory recording and control, accounts payable management and payroll processing, to name just a few. Some go as far as ERP or Enterprise Resources Planning, which includes a number of extra features that integrate some, most or all of the "back office" functions into a single platform. These functions can include product and production planning, scheduling, materials planning and purchasing, inventory control, distribution, accounting, and even many human resources functions like payroll. These systems are complex but are becoming essential for large organizations and enterprises. The emphasis is on the enterprise; the total operation whether it is manufacturing, retailing, finance, or not for profit operations and foundations.

Some complex systems can automate the ordering, receiving, payment functions, payroll records and check writing, and many others that are frequently done manually.

One important feature all systems should be to provide automatic generation of the various ratios and measures discussed in the previous chapter, both instantaneously and with trend analysis. Systems that are more sophisticated allow managers to examine the trends in these ratios and indicators from their own desk, as desired.

Chapter 15 - Time Value of Money - Present Value Concepts

One very fundamental concept in accounting, personal life and business in general is that of the Time Value of Money. We all would prefer money today rather than the promise of money in the future. Businesses, however, do not always have the cash available to make critical investments when needed. They may need to borrow the funds in order to make the investment, which is intended to increase the revenue or decrease costs.

We all recognize that there is a relationship between time and the value of money. That relationship is mathematically modeled with the concept of present value. This is not a difficult concept to understand and compute but for complex cases, the manual computation is time consuming and can lead to errors. Fortunately, computer spreadsheet programs can do all of the computations for us. We just need to properly understand and describe the problem in correct terms.

The basic notion of Present Value is that the value of something sometime in the future is not as great as its value today. Economists, engineers and accountants model this difference mathematically through the various equations to calculate present value. For example, an investment in a new machine may reduce manufacturing costs, but the firm must pay for the new machine. It will generate a series of annual cost savings that have some present value. In order to evaluate this project, we use Present Value mathematics. (See the example with Modern Manufacturing below.)

To accomplish that, we will introduce some new definitions. For several of these, we will provide illustrations.

Present Value (P); the value of an asset now, today or the amount of investment proposed.

The present value of a $100 bill is $100. The present value of a new machine proposed to be purchased is the amount of money to acquire, deliver and install the machine.

Future Value (F); the value of an asset at some selected time in the future, which may be expressed in days, months or even years. If we have some positive interest rate, this will be larger than the present value.

An amount of money deposited in a Certificate of Deposit at 5% annual interest will have a future value larger than the original deposit depending upon the amount deposited and the number of years left on deposit. Thus, for an amount of $1000 at 5% annual interest will be worth $1050 at the end of one year.

Interest Rate (i); the rate, which is associated with the passage of time for a specified asset. This may be for example, the interest charged on a credit card by the card issuer or the rate paid by an investment like a certificate of deposit. **The interest rate is the relationship between time and money**.

Number of Time Periods (n); the number of periods being considered, for example 24 months, 5 years, and so forth. The time period must agree with the interest rate. If the period is 1 month, the interest rate must be expressed as rate per month. This is extremely important since in the computation, if this rule is not followed, the output will be false.

Periodic Payment (A); for a case in which the payments are made periodically, this represents the number of payments to be made. These may be monthly, annually or whatever is consistent with n and i, or the periodic savings resulting from an investment.

Net Present Value (NPV); this is the present value of an investment made with periodic returns (A) at a specified interest rate and number of periods minus the amount of the investment to acquire the asset.

Here are some examples of the decisions made based on the Present Value model. Modern Manufacturing has the opportunity to install automation that will have the effect of reducing labor costs by $25,000 per year. This amount was determined by the engineers and the CFO is confident it is accurate. The automation will cost $55,000 to acquire, install and launch. They expect it to last at least 8 years. To evaluate this project, we need to determine the net present value (NPV) for this project. If the NPV is positive, we will save that amount of money over the eight-year period. Remember that NPV accounts for the investment as well as the resulting savings.

We regard the P value for the project to be $55,000, with $25,000 as the value for A, the periodic return and the firm uses an interest rate of 14% to evaluate these projects.

We enter an Excel® spreadsheet with those values and determine the NPV to be

$57,082. That is determined by accounting for the i = 0.14, 8 annual savings of $25,000 each and the initial investment of $55,000, using an Excel® spreadsheet. The Present Value of this savings stream is $112,082. By subtracting the initial investment of $55,000, we arrive at the Net Present Value, $57,082.

Therefore, the decision to make the investment is a good one. However, this decision must be compared with any other projects that are competing for the organization's capital funds, and any other considerations not included such as effects on productivity.

This is important because very few if any organizations have sufficient capital resources to take advantage of all their opportunities. Present value considerations are an important tool for organizations to decide how to deploy scarce assets.

Cost of Capital

As we have seen in the three important documents; i.e. the Balance Sheet, the Income Statement and the Cash Flow Statement, we need to invest money to improve and expand our business. We may borrow that money from external lenders in the form of loans, mortgages or bonds. We will have to pay for those funds at some agreed upon interest rate.

Alternatively, we could sell stock in the firm to raise capital. When we do that, our investors will expect a return for letting us use their money, so we may have to pay dividends to the stockholders.

Our third alternative is to have the owners invest more money, but again, our owners will expect a return on their investment. Money is never free, unless we generate it through profits, and we may need to invest in assets in order to generate more profits.

Cost of Capital is the cost that the firm has to pay to get the capital it uses. This is applies to both equity and debt capital and includes interest, dividends and payments for preferred stocks as well as returns to owners.

Determining the cost of these alternatives is important and we term that cost the "Cost of Capital." Mathematically, cost of capital is the weighted average of all our sources of funds, from owners, lenders or stockholders.

Example using Modern Manufacturing

Modern Manufacturing is a publicly owned company whose stock is traded on the New York Stock Exchange. The stock is currently valued at $22. Modern pays an annual dividend of $1.50 for a rate of 3.3 percent at the current share price. There are currently 50,000 shares outstanding.

They have an outstanding long-term loan of $4,000,000 at an interest rate of 8% and for new investments, they are paying 9.5% interest. They do not plan to borrow more at this time.

The founders of the firm hold Preferred Stock shares, which pay a dividend of 6%, and there are 45,000 shares outstanding at a current price of $75.

Source	Total Amount ($000's)	Percentage	Annual Cost ($000's)
Common Stock	1,100.	3.3%	36.3
Preferred Stock	1,650	6%	99.
Loans	4,000	8%	320.
Total Funding	6,750		455.3
Weighted Average Cost of Capital		6.75%	

This analysis tells us that the weighted average cost of capital is 6.75%. That means that any discretionary investment must pay back at least that amount. In order to provide a floor for new capital investments the management has set a minimum rate or hurdle rate of 14%. Any proposed capital project must be discounted at the hurdle rate. Modern Manufacturing has chosen 14% as their minimum IRR. Any project which does not meet or exceed this rate will not be approved.

Internal Rate of Return

Another way to look at these decisions is to determine the discount rate which makes the NPV equal to zero. This is called the "Internal Rate of Return" or IRR. This rate must be greater than the cost of capital and the higher the better. IRR is commonly used to compare projects that are competing for the scarce capital funds. Internal rate of return computations are not simple but fortunately, spreadsheet programs can compute it directly. IRR is presently the strongest means to evaluate capital projects. However, this is true for discretionary investments. If an investment must be made because of some situation for which the firm has no choice, such as regulatory compliance or safety issues, the firm will work hard to engineer the least expensive solution and will accept whatever IRR is determined.

Payback Period

Payback Period is another, simpler way to look at investments. It ignores the time value concept. It just looks at the investment, and determines how long it will take to pay back the investment.

Using the example above for Modern Manufacturing, the total amount to be saved over the 8 years is 8*$25,000 or $200,000. Based on an investment of $55,000, the investment will be paid back in 3.64 years. We can see that in terms of present value, the payback method overstates the present value of the investment by nearly $90,000. ($200,000 - 112,082 = $87918.) This clearly demonstrates the importance of considering present value considerations in making these decisions.

Conclusion

Our objective in this book was to introduce readers who are not accountants to the fundamental concepts and vocabulary of the world of accounting.

We have explained that the product of accounting is information. Information is needed by owners, managers, supervisors, employees, investors and all the other stakeholders. The various regulatory and taxing authorities are important members of this group of stakeholders.

A number of accounting positions are described along with the education and training required for them.

We have explained and discussed the three important reports produced by the accounting office; the Income Statement, the Balance Sheet and the Cash Flow Statement. The examples for these reports and statements illustrate their important contents.

Further, we have introduced some commonly used methods to evaluate the information reported, in terms of position, income, efficiency and strength for the organization. Appendix 1 includes an example case with the results for many of these ratios and measures.

We trust that this book has met your expectations. It was not intended to make the reader an accountant but rather, to introduce the profession and practice of accounting and point out how management and other stakeholders use this information for planning and decision making.

Appendix 1

Barksdale Construction is a large developer of commercial and residential properties. The owners invested $250,000 to start the company a number of years ago and then expanded their financing by selling preferred stock at an 8% dividend rate. This means that Preferred Dividends must be paid before any other payments from earnings, that is the preferred stockholders have priority over the other owners. The company has not sold any common stock so it is not considered publicly owned.

The last section contains several commonly used ratios and measures for Barksdale Construction. No judgment is made since these measures are most important when compared with budget, prior periods and common industry results. Interested parties will use these results to draw judgments about the firm and compare these results with similar firms in the same industry.

BALANCE SHEET
BARKSDALE CONSTRUCTION COMPANY, INC.

Asset/Liability	$	$
Current Assets		
Cash and Marketable Securities	180,000	
Accounts Receivable	43,000	
Inventories	125,000	
Total Current Assets		348,000
Land and Buildings	248,000	
Equipment	310,000	
Accumulated Depreciation	105,000	
Investments and Undeveloped Property	540,000	
Intangibles	16,000	
Total Long Term Assets		1,219,000
Total Assets		1,567,000
Liabilities		
Accounts Payable	25,000	
Taxes Payable	15,000	
Dividends Payable	14,000	
Total Current Liabilities		54,000
Preferred Stock	674,000	
Notes Payable	180,000	
Mortgages Payable	252,000	
Invested Capital	250,000	
Retained Earnings	157,000	
Total Owners Equity		1,513,000
Total Liabilities and Equity		1,567,000

INCOME STATEMENT
BARKSDALE CONSTRUCTION COMPANY, INC.
Year Ended December 31, 2015

Revenue/Disbursements	$	$
Sales	2,368,500	
Less Uncollectibles	(5,280)	
Gross Revenue	2,363,220	
Operating Expenses		
Cost of Goods Sold	1,368,000	
Wages and Salaries	357,370	
Supplies Expense	2,895	
Insurance Premiums	23,000	
Depreciation Expense	35,400	
General and Administrative	37,890	
Property Taxes	48,750	
Total Operating Expenses	1,837,905	
Operating Profit	525,315	
Other Expenses		
Dividends Paid	24,500	
Interest Expense	2,470	
Profit Before Taxes	498,345	
Income Taxes	174,421	
Net Profit	498,345	

Measures and Ratios for Barksdale Construction Company

Equity to Liability Ratio	$461,000/$1,567,000 = 0.30
Times Interest Earned	$525,315/$26,970 = 19.48
Debt to Equity Ratio	$1,160,000/$407,000 = 2.85
Current Ratio	$348,000/$54,000 = 6.45
Receivables Turnover	$2,363,220/$1,219,000 = 54.96
Turnover of Assets	$2,363,220/$$1,219,000 = 1.94
Operating Ratio	$1,802,505/$$2,363,220 = 0.77
Return on Investment (ROI)	$560,715/$1,567,000 = 41%
Return on Equity (ROE)	$560,715/$1,513,000 = 37%
Return on Capital Employed (ROCE)	$560,715/$1,513,000 = 37%

Made in United States
North Haven, CT
18 October 2022

25612059R00057